Art Quilt Finishing Essentials

How to Bind, Display, Label, Store & Care for your Art Quilts

DEBORAH WIRSU

Copyright © 2019 Deborah Wirsu
All rights reserved. No part of this publication may be reproduced, stored in a retrieval system or transmitted in any form or by any means, electronic, mechanical, photocopying, recording, scanning, or otherwise without the written permission of the copyright owner.
Legal Disclaimer: This book contains techniques, strategies and advice that may not produce the same results for you. The author makes no representations or warranties with respect to the accuracy or completeness of the contents of this book. The advice and strategies contained in this book may not be suitable for you or your situation. You assume sole responsibility for the outcome of any technique or strategy provided in this book.
Wirsu, Deborah
Art Quilt Finishing Essentials: How to Bind, Display, Label, Store & Care for your Art Quilts
©2019 Deborah Wirsu
All rights reserved.
ISBN-13: 9781798249789

CONTENTS

HOW TO BIND A QUILT WITH SIMPLE MITERED CORNERS	1
1.1 Introduction	2
1.2 Trim your Quilt to Size	3
1.3 Cut the Binding Strips	5
1.4 Attach the Binding Strips	8
2 HOW TO BLIND FACE A QUILT	10
2.1 Introduction	11
2.2 Prepare the facing strips	11
2.3 Attach the facings	12
3 HOW TO MAKE A HANGING SLEEVE	15
3.1 Introduction	16
3.2 Fabric for the hanging sleeve	17
3.3 Measuring and cutting	18
3.4 Stitching the pocket	18
3.5 Attaching the hanging sleeve	19
3.6 Hanging your quilt	20
4 HOW TO LABEL YOUR QUILT	21
4.1 Introduction	22
4.2 Making your Quilt Label	24
5 HOW TO MAKE AN ART QUILT TRAVEL BAG	28
5.1 Introduction	29
5.2 Materials for the travel bag	30
5.3 Constructing the travel bag	31
5.4 Finishing the travel bag	34
6 CARING FOR YOUR ART AND PATCHWORK QUILTS	35
6.1 Introduction	36
6.2 Handling your Quilt	37
6.3 Cleaning your Quilt	37
6.4 Hanging your quilt	41
6.5 Storing your quilts	42
ABOUT THE AUTHOR	44
OTHER BOOKS BY DEBORAH WIRSU	45

FORWARD

This little book – designed for newcomers to the world of art quilts, and quilts in general – guides you through six essential techniques for finishing and caring for your quilts.

So often we are given instructions about how to put together the design for a quilt, stitching techniques, and so on, but are never enlightened about how to finish, display and care for our precious works of art once they're complete.

Art quilts can be bound or finished in myriad ways, and the two most common ways are outlined here, along with details on simple ways to display and travel with your quilt. After all, you want to take it to shows and competitions, don't you, to show off your new creation!

- How to Bind a Quilt with Simple Mitered Corners
- How to Blind Face a Quilt
- How to make a Hanging Sleeve
- How to Label your Quilt
- How to make a Quilt Travel Bag
- How to Care for your Art & Patchwork Quilts

Using these techniques allows your work to be completed professionally and in style.

HOW TO BIND A QUILT WITH SIMPLE MITERED CORNERS

Single fold binding with mitered corners – in 4 easy steps

1.1 INTRODUCTION

Binding a quilt need not be the challenging experience that some people imagine it to be, and doing it yourself is rewarding, as you can achieve exactly the look you want.

There are many ways to bind quilts, with the traditional method being to create double-fold binding with mitered corners.

Art quilts do not always require the extra bulk of double-fold binding so modifying this traditional approach to use a **single fold**, still with mitered corners, gives your art quilts a neat and professional finish.

Double fold binding is beautiful, and indeed very practical for bed quilts or those exposed to a lot of wear and tear. However, the rough and tumble of handling is not something art quilts are generally exposed to. In addition, the extra bulk of double-fold binding does not always complement a piece of art designed for hanging or framing.

Single fold binding, constructed from the same, toning or contrasting fabric as the quilt top, allows the quilt to hang straight.

Follow these 4 easy steps and your quilt will be bound in a flash, and look stunning, as well!

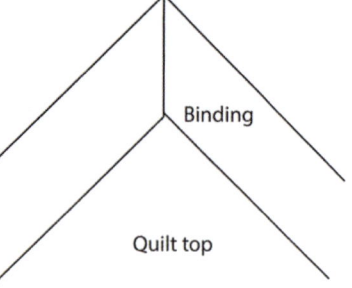

1.2 TRIM YOUR QUILT TO SIZE

Trimming is, perhaps, the only step in the process where you could make a ***major*** (and potentially irreversible) error, so take care here! Once you have straightened and trimmed, the edges are gone!

Once cut, you can't 'un-cut'!

Repairing an error like this can be challenging and may result in your quilt ending up with a completely different look to your original intentions.

Do not cut anything until you're sure of your measurements!

MEASURE TWICE — CUT ONCE

Square Up

The process of quilting a surface, especially if it has heavy embellishments or dense thread painting, can cause the edges of a quilt to 'change shape' during stitching, resulting in uneven side lengths, and pulling in of the sides.

Begin by marking the center of your quilt. Place it on a flat surface, preferably on a self-healing cutting mat with grid-lines marked (if you have one large enough), and marking the midway point — vertically and horizontally — of the quilt. Use a quilter's or dressmaker's square and erasable fabric marker to do this.

Mark the outer perimeter of the quilt, making sure each corner forms an exact right angle (unless you have specifically planned an irregular or free-form edge). Marking the straight edges with an erasable quilt marker makes checking the angles much easier.

TIP: Mark the outer perimeter of what will be the *finished size* of the quilt (including binding). Then create another marker *inside* that square, which indicates the attachment or stitching line for the binding.

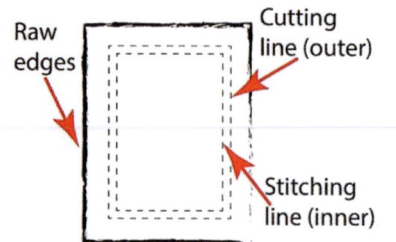

To determine how far inside to mark this second set of lines, you should consider **how wide you want your binding to be**.

For narrow binding — say ½" — you should mark the inside square or rectangle ½" inside the outer square, while wide binding — 3" for instance — would result in the inner square (or rectangle) being 3" inside the *outer* line.

Ideally, this is something you will have planned from the outset, to ensure that you have left sufficient fabric around your design to create the desired width of edging.

Using a cutting mat, rotary cutter and quilter's ruler, cut away the excess fabric (top, batting and backing), cutting along the *outer* line.

Measure

Measure each outside edge of the quilt.

If your quilt is rectangular in shape, then the upper and lower edges will be matching, as will the left and right edges.

If your quilt is square, then each side should be the same length.
Write down your measurements. You will need these to determine how much binding to cut.

1.3 CUT THE BINDING STRIPS

Your preferred width of binding will determine how wide you cut the fabric strips.

Formula for calculating width of strips

With single-fold binding you will need enough fabric to cover the width of binding on the front and back of your quilt, plus ½" seam allowance (1/4" on each long side).

Width of strips = (Width of binding x 2) + (seam allowance x 2)

Formula for calculating length of strips

The length of strips is easy to calculate, as you need sufficient to extend right around your quilt. Keep in mind that mitering the corners takes up additional fabric, so allow at least an extra 20" of length to your calculation.

Better to have too much length than not enough!

Length of strips = Sum of length of all sides + 20"

Sample directions for making a 1/4" binding

Using the same fabric as your quilt (or your edging fabric of choice), cut binding strips ½" wide.

This was calculated as follows:

(Width of binding x 2) + (seam allowance x 2) = Width of strips

(1/2" x 2) +(1/2" x 2) = 2"

If the sides of your quilt are straight, cut the strips on the *straight grain* of the fabric.

If the sides of your quilt are curved, cut the strips on the *diagonal grain* to form bias strips. Mitering corners on irregularly-shaped quilts can pose additional problems, so this method is best for straight-sided quilts.

Cut enough lengths of fabric that, when stitched together (end to end), they will reach around all sides of your quilt. Unless the quilt is very small, you will probably have to join the strips.

Joining straight-grain strips

To join binding strips cut on the straight grain, join the strips together until you have sufficient length to reach around all sides of your quilt, plus at least 20".

Take the ends of two strips and lay them across each other, right sides together, at right angles, as shown.

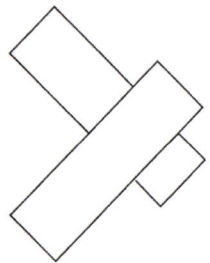

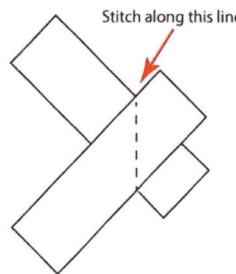

Mark the diagonal where the strips cross, and **stitch** across that line with a ¼" seam.

Trim the seam allowance and press open.

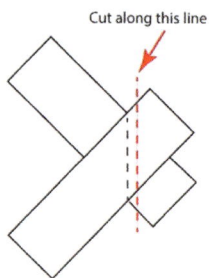

Joining bias-grain strips

Cut one end of two different strips on the diagonal.

Aligning the edges, place the two strips, right sides together, so that the narrow-angle corners extend ¼" beyond the other strip. The two strips should form a right angle.

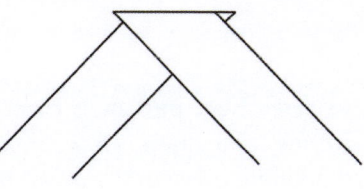

Stitch across the ends with a ¼" seam.

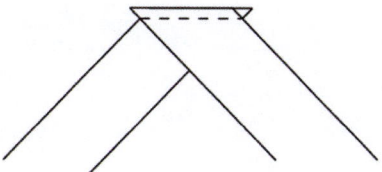

Open the strips out, press the seam open and trim the corners that extend beyond the edges.

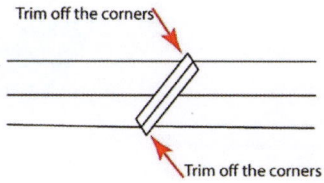

Trim off the corners

Trim off the corners

1.4 ATTACH THE BINDING STRIPS

Fold one short end of a binding strip on the diagonal, wrong sides together, and press. This conceals the raw edge when the binding is turned. (The other end will not be folded).

Pin this folded end to your quilt, placing the right side of the binding strip against the right side of the quilt (the top or face or your quilt), aligning the raw edges.

Begin your stitching several inches along the binding strip, using a ½" seam allowance, sewing until you reach ½" from the next corner.

Back-stitch to secure the threads, then cut the threads.

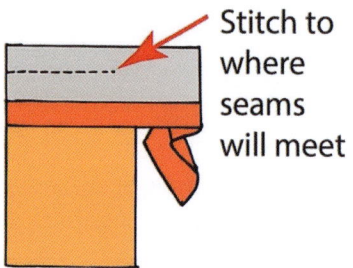

Stitch to where seams will meet

N.B. If your binding is wider, stop stitching when you reach the same distance from the corner as the width of your seam allowance.

Make the mitered corner by folding the loose binding diagonally up from the corner (it will be triangular in shape).

Stitch across the diagonal line formed by this fold. Very narrow binding can be left unstitched across the diagonal.

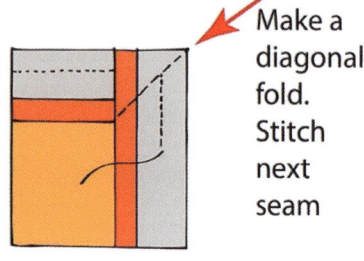

Make a diagonal fold. Stitch next seam

Now, beginning where the first stitched seam ended, **stitch** along the next edge, stopping again, ½" from the next corner.

Repeat the process for each corner.

Joining the ends

As you approach the end of stitching the binding, **stop stitching about 3–5"** from where you started and secure with backstitching.

Trim the excess binding, allowing sufficient fabric to overlap where you began by several inches.

Leaving the second end unfolded, **layer** it over the beginning by about ½". **Pin securely**.

Resume stitching from where you last stopped, until you have overlapped where you began.

Finishing

Finger press the 'triangle' of fabric that forms the miter so that the 'fold' is now aligned diagonally across the facing, lying flat to each side of the diagonal.

Fold the binding to the back of your quilt, **turning** the long raw edges under ½", pin the binding in position, and hand stitch to the back of your quilt.

Fold binding to back, forming neat miter at the same time

Mitered corners can be a little fiddly at first. Just take your time, measure twice, check your angles, and you will achieve neat, mitered corners. Once you've tried this technique a few times, it becomes a comfortable process.

2 HOW TO BLIND FACE A QUILT

The pillow-case method – neat, sleek and contemporary

2.1 INTRODUCTION

Contemporary quilts can be greatly enhanced by being finished *without* a visible border. This gives them a contemporary appearance that is popular with art quilters in the 21st century and is also suitable for irregularly-shaped quilts.

Blind facing is really very easy. Although it is somewhat similar to attaching conventional binding, you don't need to worry about those potentially tricky mitered corners!

Choose fabric that blends or tones well with the top or face of your quilt, so that it becomes almost unnoticeable when complete.

If you're having difficulty selecting an appropriate fabric, or the top of your quilt is very multi-colored, select the dominant dark color on the quilt. **Dark colors recede** more than light, and our eyes are less drawn to dark shades.

2.2 PREPARE THE FACING STRIPS

Trim your Quilt to Size

To square up your quilt, see ***Trim your Quilt to Size*** in **Part One.**

Using an erasable fabric marker, or quilting chalk, **mark the *outer* boundary of your *finished* quilt**, making sure the corners are squared and the sides parallel.

Then draw another marker line ¼" *outside* **the first line.**

Using a rotary cutter and quilt ruler, **trim the quilt along the *outer* line** Do not make the mistake of cutting along the *inner* line.

Measure the length of the upper and lower edges, and both sides.

Prepare the Facing Strips

Cut four strips of facing fabric, each measuring:

1 ½" wide x length of side

If your quilt is rectangular in shape, you will have two pieces the length of the upper/lower edges of your quilt, and two pieces the length of the sides.

If your quilt is square, you will have four pieces, each the same, matching the length of the sides.

Press under ¼" on one *long* edge of each facing strip, turning the fold towards the back, wrong sides together.

2.3 ATTACH THE FACINGS

Attaching the Upper and Lower Facings

With wrong sides and raw (unfolded) edges together, place an appropriate strip along the top edge of your quilt. Pin in position.

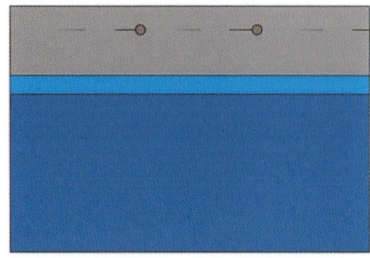

Beginning at one turned edge, **stitch a ¼" seam**, stopping ¼" from the corner.

Stop in the 'needle down' position, pivot the quilt and continue stitching along the next edge, stopping again ¼" from the next corner.

Once again, **pivot and continue** until you reach the turned edge.
Repeat this process for the lower edge of your quilt.

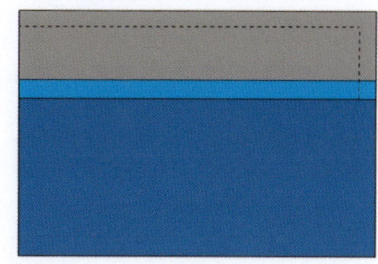

Attaching the Side Facings

Pin each side strip to the quilt, place the short edge so that it overlaps the top and bottom strips by about ¼" – ½", to cover the folded edge.

Stitch along the side edges, using a ¼" seam, stopping when the side strips overlap the facing strip on the next edge.

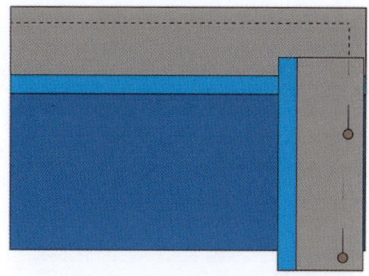

Work a backstitch to secure the ends, then trim off any excess fabric length.

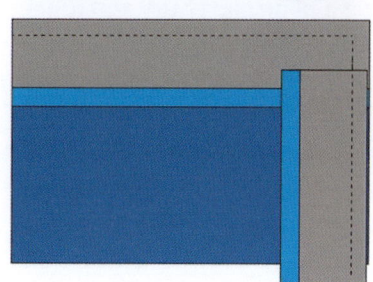

Finishing

Trim Corners, Turn and Pin

Trim diagonally across each corner to reduce the fabric bulk, as this would create a lumpy corner when the pocket is turned.

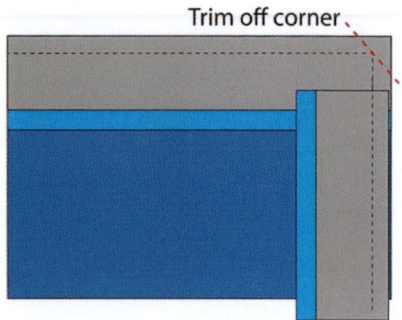

Now **turn** all the facings to the back of the quilt.

You'll notice that attaching the facings in this manner has resulted in the creation of a **'pocket'** at each corner.

It may be necessary to use a pencil or knitting needle to push the corners out, to make them square, and eliminate any folds or tucks in the seams.

Hand stitch the folded edge

Finish the facing by hand-stitching the folded hem in place on the back, using a blind slip stitch and toning thread.

Blind facing quilts is so easy and results in a wonderful, contemporary look.

3 HOW TO MAKE A HANGING SLEEVE

Hang your quilts in style!

3.1 INTRODUCTION

Quilts are no longer simply functional, though decorative, items used to keep us warm at night.

The art quilt 'revolution' of the past 30 years or so has seen many of us wanting to display our creativity on walls and in galleries.

And it's not only art quilts that are being hung on walls. So many creative stitchers make such beautiful 'patchwork' quilts (for want of a better term) that they are reluctant to use them in everyday life, and therefore display them as 'art' instead by hanging them on a wall.

In addition, entering a quilt of almost any type in a quilting competition or show requires that it has a hanging sleeve attached to the back prior to delivery to the venue.

There are a number of ways to prepare a quilt for display, with the simple hanging sleeve being the most popular. This method is excellent if you think you may wish to remove the hanging sleeve at some time in the future, as it is attached by hand, rather than stitched into the binding.

This method is also very easy!

3.2 FABRIC FOR THE HANGING SLEEVE

Any strong, non-stretch fabric can be used; however, cotton or calico is usually the most appropriate, and easiest to work with.

As the hanging sleeve is hidden away at the back of your quilt, the color of the fabric you use is really up to you.

However, if you want your quilt to look professional — keeping in mind that quilting competition judges look at the *back* of your work as well as the front — then opt to use either the same fabric as the quilt backing, or a toning shade of plain fabric.

Keep in mind, too, that darker colors are less 'visible' than light or bright colors.

This is just one of many ways to hang a quilt. Nevertheless, this method is quick, easy and very effective.

3.3 MEASURING AND CUTTING

Measure the width of your quilt along the top edge and cut a piece of fabric that measures:

Width of quilt x 10" deep

Be sure to cut this fabric on the *straight grain*. Any deviation from that will cause a slight bias in the fabric, resulting in it sagging or stretching out of shape. If this occurs, your quilt will not hang straight when displayed.

3.4 STITCHING THE POCKET

Turn under the two **short** sides ¼" (**wrong sides together**) then turn again a further ½". **Press.**

Secure each of these folds using regular straight, machine stitching.

This creates a neat edge at each end of the pocket, and, being sealed neatly, will not 'catch' on the hanging rod or batten when it's inserted. Fold the rectangle in half lengthwise, ***wrong sides together.***

Stitch the raw edges together along the ***long edge*** using a 5/8" seam. Press seam open.

Position the seam so that it is at the center back of the pocket when pressed flat. Press the sleeve folds.

Notice that I have not turned the sleeve. With the open seam now lying against the back of the quilt, it will not be seen, and therefore won't interfere when the rod or batten is inserted.

3.5 ATTACHING THE HANGING SLEEVE

In order to give your hanging sleeve a little 'wriggle room', to accommodate the rod or batten, **roll the top layer** of your sleeve about ¼" from one of the creased folds.

Lightly press (or 'finger press') this second fold.

Your hanging sleeve should now be flat on the 'seam' side and puffed out a little (like a D-ring) on the other side.

Position the long top edge of the sleeve on the back of your quilt, equidistant from each edge and set down approximately ¾" from the top of the quilt binding.

How far you position the sleeve from the top does depend a little on the size of the quilt and the size of the hanging rod to be used. A thick dowel rod will need more wriggle room than a flat batten.

Hand stitch the top edge of the sleeve to the back of the quilt, using a firm slip stitch.

Pin the lower edge in place, making sure you use the soft crease that introduced fullness to the sleeve.

Hand stitch the lower edge of the sleeve.

Hand slip-stitch the back edges (the side with the seam) of the sleeve lightly to the quilt at each end, to avoid having someone place a hanging rod through the wrong part of the sleeve.

3.6 HANGING YOUR QUILT

Decide where you want to display your quilt and insert a picture hook into the wall.

If your quilt is very large, then you may need to use two picture hooks, for strength and balance — one towards each side of the quilt.

Insert a rod or batten then attach a length of strong cord or picture wire to each end of the rod, just as you would if hanging a framed picture. Your quilt is now ready to go on display!

4 HOW TO LABEL YOUR QUILT

Don't let your work get lost in time

4.1 INTRODUCTION

Your quilt is finished and it's ready to use or display. Complete at last! It's a very satisfying feeling. But wait just a moment! You're not done yet.

Documenting your work is an important part of the finishing process, just as is binding and creating a hanging sleeve.

Thanks to modern technology, there are many options for making a quilt label. Elegant computer-printed labels, pre-printed labels and custom-embroidered labels are all available. It really comes down to personal preference.

It's worth taking the time to make a lovely label. Don't you think your children or grandchildren would gain great joy from knowing all the details of how the quilt came to be made, especially if it was for them?

Factors influencing how you label a quilt include:
- Who is the recipient?
- What will the quilt be used for?
- Has it been entered (or is it likely to be in the future) in a competition or exhibition?
- Are you after a formal or informal and friendly appearance?

Why document your quilts

Through history, artists have nearly always signed their paintings, generally in a lower corner, and sometimes including the date. Many signatures have since become famous and very recognizable — Monet, Van Gogh, Picasso ...

In China and other regions of Asia, 'signatures' were often applied in the form of a **carved stamp** — known as a **chop seal** — dipped in red ink or cinnabar paste. These seals are typically carved from stone, and also wood, metal and plastic. In the past, ivory was also used — worldwide restrictions on the use of ivory have now ended this practice. The one I have is carved into soft stone.

Sadly, labelling and documenting quilts has not always been a tradition, but fortunately, quilters and textile artists have now taken to recording relevant information about their work, using labels attached to the back, or underside (in the case of 3D textile pieces).

Some textile artists also choose to sign their work by **embroidering or writing their name** on the front of their quilt, as you would see on a painting, or hand-signing on the label on the back.

Visit any museum or gallery where antique and heirloom quilts are displayed and there is often no record of the maker, or even where and when a quilt was made, or *why* it was made.

This is a great shame as it leads to historians having to make educated 'guesses', based on extensive research, regarding the origins of some historical works.

Textile historians can glean much information from the fabric itself, designs used, and stitching techniques. But how much more wonderful it is if you can also learn the *history* of a particular work, and gain insight into the life and times of the person who made it.

Recording relevant information about your work preserves its provenance for future generations, potentially increasing the value of a piece or collection as well. It's worth preserving the provenance of anything you collect — old photos in your possession, ceramics, books, and so on.

4.2 MAKING YOUR QUILT LABEL

What information should the label contain?

The minimum information on a quilt label should include:
- The name of the quilt (if any).
- Your name.
- The date the quilt was made.

Other information you should consider adding includes:
- Where the quilt was made.
- Why it was made. Was it as a gift? If so, for whom? Does it celebrate a special occasion or event (wedding, birth, memorial)? Has it been made for a special exhibit or competition?
- Some people like to include special quotes — a piece of verse, or a quote from the Bible or other meaningful texts are popular.
- The dimensions of the quilt.
- Types of fabric included.

- Construction method and stitching techniques.
- Any other techniques, such as fabric painting.
- A photo of the quilt. These days, it's easy to print images on fabric, using ordinary home printers. Using the correct materials will ensure the image stays true over time.

It really is important to consider what people may want to know about your quilt, both now and in the future.

Making Your Quilt Label

Two options for label-making:

Basic labels

Very basic labels require few supplies:
- Small piece of fabric, square or rectangular, cut to about 4"x4" or 4"x 6".
- Permanent marking pen

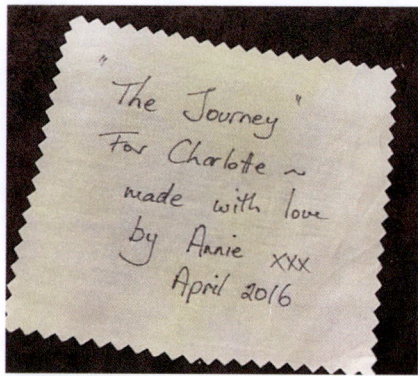

Write the desired information on the piece of fabric.

Fold each side border to the back (wrong sides together), tucking under ¼". Press.

Or simply cut with pinking shears, as in the photo.

Slip stitch the label to the back of your quilt by hand.

Computer-printed labels

'Moroccan Spice'

DEBORAH WIRSU
© March 2014

15" x 15"
Hand painted cotton,
raw edge appliqué,
machine quilting
Theme: *Love*

www.ThreadSketchingInAction.com

Prepare the label text

Using a standard text editor (e.g. Word, Apple Pages), or a program such as Adobe Photoshop or Illustrator (if you're familiar with their use and have them installed on your computer):

- Create a text box
- Type the desired information inside the text box. Use a large enough font that the print will be easy to read when printed on fabric.
- Add a photo image of your quilt, if desired. This allows for quick recognition of a work.

Prepare the fabric

These methods work well if you have several labels to make, as up to 4 will fit on a standard A4 or US Letter size printer page.

Alternatively, position the printout so that it prints at the top or bottom of your page. This way, the rest of the fabric can be used later, reducing wastage.

Then, EITHER:

Use a commercial printable fabric sheet, **OR:**

- Cut a piece of plain cotton fabric a little larger than a standard printer page.
- Cut a piece of paper-backed fusible web to fit the fabric.
- Fuse the fusible web to the back of the fabric, using a hot iron.
- Trim to standard printer size (A4 or US Letter).

THEN:

- Insert in your printer's paper feed tray.
- Make sure the text is aligned on the page as you want, prior to printing.
- Print.
- Trim the fabric to the size of the text box, allowing ¼" extra fabric on each side, to turn under.
- Remove the paper backing from the fusible web (or the backing paper of commercial printable fabric sheet).
- Turn under the allowances (wrong sides together) on the label.
- Pin or fuse the label (with allowances turned under) to the back of your quilt.
- Slip stitch the edges.

OR:

- Follow the same general guidelines, using freezer paper to stabilize the fabric as it runs through the printer.
- Fold the allowances under each edge. Press.
- Slip stitch the label in position on the back of your quilt.

5 HOW TO MAKE AN ART QUILT TRAVEL BAG

Reusable travel or storage bag for your treasured quilts

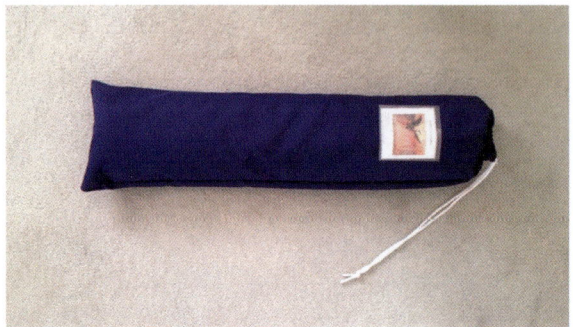

5.1 INTRODUCTION

Entering your art quilt in a quilt show or challenge generally requires you to deliver your quilt in a custom travel or storage bag. While some people elect to use over-sized tote bags, unless these are sealed, it is easy for your quilt to become soiled or possibly even damaged during transport.

A dedicated travel bag not only makes it easier for the curators to store or transport your quilt, but also keeps your treasured quilt in pristine condition during this process.

Many quilt bags are made to a square or rectangular shape, requiring the quilt to be folded before placing it in the bag. With many patchwork quilts this is not a major problem, as the quilts are often large, and any creases fall out once the quilt is hung, or the creases can be lightly steamed out with an iron.

But when it comes to art quilts, folding is often not suitable, and, on occasions, not possible, due to the quilt's construction.

Would you really want to fold your stunning work of art that you've spent months or years creating, with all its details and embellishments?

Perhaps your art quilt is too stiff from layers of stabilizers and stitching to even fold successfully, without damaging the surface of the quilt.

In addition, art quilts often don't comply to standard sizes, and many certainly do not fit into a standard quilt travel tote bag.

If this is the case with your quilt — whether it be an art quilt or a more traditional format — then *rolling* **the quilt** is generally the solution.
If your quilt also can't be rolled, this necessitates the brainstorming of an even more creative solution! (e.g. a bag large enough to hold the quilt without rolling or folding).

In order to store or transport *rolled quilts*, I've created the **Quilt Traveler** — a simple art quilt travel bag designed specifically for **rolled quilts**.

It's possible to whip up several of these in an afternoon, and if you make them in a number of different sizes, you'll always have a travel bag on hand for your quilts.

The Quilt Traveler is offered here in 3 different sizes, but creating your own custom size is easy once you understand the formula and construction method.

Let's get started making a Quilt Traveler or two!

5.2 MATERIALS FOR THE TRAVEL BAG

Fabric

These bags are very inexpensive to make, however, opt for **sturdy fabric** where possible, rather than plain muslin or quilter's cotton, as these offer little support. It is more challenging to get your quilt in and out of the bag if it has no inherent strength of its own, and it also doesn't offer a great deal of protection from knocks, stacking or bad weather.

Fabric such as cotton canvas, cotton duck or sturdy nylon (for instance, the fabric used for many heavy, windproof jackets) are a good choice. They offer protection for your quilt, and even a little water-resistance in case you need to carry your quilt through the odd rain-shower going from car to venue.

I use weather-resistant cotton canvas for my quilt bags. Cotton canvas is relatively inexpensive, easy to sew, has inherent strength and stability, and my quilts slide in and out of the bag with ease.

What you need

This pattern makes 3 bags — **Small, Medium and Medium/Large**, using the measurements given below.

- 1 yard/meter sturdy cotton canvas, cotton duck or nylon — 55" (140 cm) wide.
- 2.5 yards/meters cotton or nylon draw cord.
- 3 x spring-loaded cord fastener
- 3 x plastic photo pocket
- Thread and general sewing supplies — scissors, pins, sewing machine, etc.

5.3 CONSTRUCTING THE TRAVEL BAG

Cutting

Cut **3 rectangles of fabric** (or cut to your custom size — see Formula below).

Small –16" x 24"
Medium –20" x 34"
Med/Large –25" x 45"

Custom Sizing

Make to your own requirements! Here's how to do it …

Roll your quilt and measure the **length** and **circumference** of the roll.

Formula

For each custom bag, cut one rectangle of fabric that measures:
(Circumference + 4") x (Length + 8")

Attach the plastic photo pocket.

Position the plastic photo pocket in a prominent position on your Traveler and, using a slightly longer than usual stitch length, stitch down along 3 sides, leaving the pocket opening unstitched. Backstitch a couple of stitches at the beginning and end to secure the stitching.

The reasoning behind the longer stitch length is that machining plastic — even quite firm plastic — renders it liable to tearing or splitting, so it's better not to put more stitch holes in it than necessary.

Neaten the raw edges

Using zigzag stitch or serge stitch, **neaten the raw edges** on the sides and lower edges of the bag, to prevent fraying.

Stitch the side seam

Fold the rectangle lengthwise, right sides together and pin the lower and side seam. Leave the top of the bag open!

Stitch the lower and side seam using a 5/8" seam.

Turn the bag right side out. Insert your hand into the bag and pull from the inside to turn it so that the right side of the fabric is now on the outside.

Make the draw cord pocket

Fold the top edge to the inside, using a ¼" fold. Press.

Fold this edge to the inside **again**, using a 1" fold. Press.

Pin the folded edge to the bag.

Top stitch the folded edge to secure in position, leaving a small opening for inserting the draw cord.

Top stitch again, 1/8" from the top edge of the bag.

Insert the draw cord and attach the cord fastener.

Cut a length of cord approximately 24" in length (longer if the circumference of your bag is bigger than the bag sizes used in this pattern).

Thread the cord through the top cord pocket using the access point you left when stitching the fold.

If you don't have a dedicated cord-inserter, use a safety pin attached to the end of the cord, and gently maneuver the cord through the pocket.

Secure the ends of the cord by either melting the ends over a candle or match (for nylon cord), or wrap a little adhesive tape around the end, to prevent fraying.

Insert the ends through the cord fastener. Tie the ends together to prevent the cord fastener from being removed.

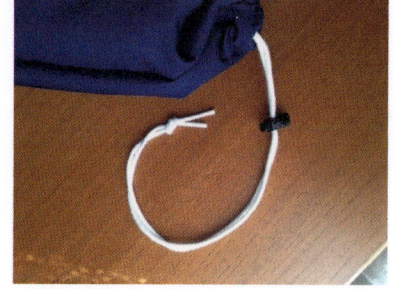

5.4 FINISHING THE TRAVEL BAG

Add a label

Write or print the details of your quilt on paper or light card.
Cut this to fit into the plastic pocket on the outside of the bag and slip it in.

The label should include:
- The name of the quilt.
- Your name and contact details (where required).

I also like to include a **photo** of the quilt, making it easy to select a particular quilt quickly, if you have a number of them stacked alongside each other.

Ready to use!

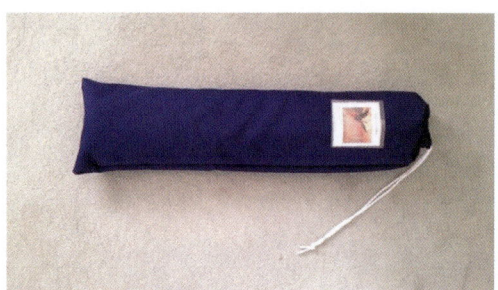

Roll your quilt (preferably **right side out**), wrap in tissue or a clean sheet (if desired) and slide it into your new Quilt Traveler bag.

Now you're read to 'hit the road', knowing your quilt is protected.

6 CARING FOR YOUR ART AND PATCHWORK QUILTS

Handling – Cleaning – Hanging – Storing

6.1 INTRODUCTION

Your quilt is a work of art

It doesn't make any difference if your art quilt is one you made to keep, give as a gift, or sell, or even if it's one you have bought or been given, it's a work of fine art and should be treated as such.

Art quilts deserve the same level of care you would give a painting or drawing. Museums and galleries the world over contain textile works that may be hundreds, or perhaps thousands of years old — natural fibers are tougher than you may imagine!

With the correct care, your quilt will outlive you, to be handed down to future generations.

Most quilts are made from durable natural fibers such cotton, wool or silk. These fibers may change over time, with exposure to light and air, but will not deteriorate greatly if cared for appropriately. Contemporary quilts, especially art quilts, often contain other fibers such as paper, plastic, metal, gilding, beads, and more!

'Everyday' quilts are subjected to the rough and tumble of children, pets, and washing machines, so folding and storing correctly will ensure they last longer and stay in better condition, if looked after with love, while antique and heirloom quilts should receive specialist care with the use of appropriate archival storage materials.

Follow these simple guidelines and your work will look just as beautiful in the future as it does now.

6.2 HANDLING YOUR QUILT

Quilts are textile items and textiles attract moisture and oils from your hands when you touch them. Your hands carry natural oils which transfer to the fabric. In turn, these oils attract dust and grime.

Over time, these oils stain and damage your quilt, leaving ugly, brown blotches and oil stains that can be difficult to remove.

Always wash your hands before handling your quilt, or wear clean, white, cotton gloves.

Art quilts, antique or heirloom quilts are best handled as little as possible. However, 'everyday', utilitarian quilts are frequently handled and so demand a different form of care.

Keep in mind that a 'patchwork' quilt, if hung on a wall and used as display, rather than placed on a bed, for example, is just as much a piece of 'art' as any work created specifically as art.

I know of many instances where intricate, high-quality patchwork quilts have been considered 'too good' to use in daily life!

6.3 CLEANING YOUR QUILT

Frequently-used handmade quilts

How you clean your quilt depends on what type of quilt it is, its texture, construction, pliability, use and location. Using a quilt on a daily basis, especially if there are children or pets in your home, will naturally lead to more soiling than would occur if the quilt were hung on the wall.

Washing

Day-to-day, utilitarian quilts are generally washed when soiled.

Unless the quilt has delicate appliqué, high-loft batting, or is made from less resistant materials, washing is the easiest way to clean these quilts.

Color-fastness

If you have never washed your quilt before, test the color-fastness of the fabric prior to washing. Be especially attentive to this process if the quilt has high-contrast colors — dark and light — as you don't want the dark colors to run or bleed.

To test color-fastness, rub the quilt fabric using a piece of hot, wet, white cotton fabric. The color from the quilt should not transfer to the white cotton. If it does, have the quilt professionally cleaned.

Washing and Drying

Many people like to wash their quilts by hand, and this is indeed, the gentlest way to do it. However, there are times when a quilt may be subjected to a great deal of use and wear from babies, children, and pets, and thus require something more.

In this instance, a domestic washing machine can be used, but very large quilts may also need to be washed in a commercial machine or taken to a dry-cleaning service that also 'washes', which most do, these days.

Wash your quilt in cold water, on a gentle cycle, using a mild, perfume-free detergent.

Add ½ cup of plain, white vinegar to the first rinse water, as this helps remove any detergent residue from the quilt prior to the final rinse.

It's best not to hang a quilt while it is drying as the weight of the water can pull the quilt out of shape and break or distort the threads. Where possible, lie the quilt flat on a table, flat clothes line, or on a sheet over a clean, dry lawn.

Choose a warm day to wash your quilt but avoid drying it in full sun as this will hasten the fading of colors.

Dry-cleaning

When it's impractical to wash your quilt, or its delicate nature requires different treatment, take your quilt to a professional drycleaner. Check their terms and conditions or ask them if they are familiar with dry-cleaning handmade quilts (as opposed to doonas, duvets or bed pillows).

Cleaning antique and heirloom quilts

Before cleaning any antique, heirloom or valuable quilt or textile art, take a good look at it, all over, to see if any repair work needs to be undertaken before cleaning. Repairs are best undertaken prior to cleaning, as the cleaning process itself may lead to more damage.

Also keep in mind that antique quilts often used hand-dyed fabrics in their construction. These dyes were generally not as color-fast as modern dyes, so be sure to test the color-fastness or err on the side of caution and do not wash the quilt!

However, depending on their use and value, even antique and heirloom quilts can be washed, preferably by hand, using liquid detergents specially developed for washing fine fabric items.

If the quilt is merely dusty, this can be removed using a vacuum cleaner. Set the vacuum cleaner to its lowest power setting and fit the upholstery or brush attachment. Gently work your way across the quilt, removing all the dust. Then hang the quilt in the fresh air—out of direct sunlight—to remove any odors or musty smells.

Avoid having an antique or heirloom quilt dry-cleaned as the chemicals used can damage the fibers and dyes in the quilt. Extremely valuable or very old quilts should be taken to a textile conservator for professional cleaning.

Cleaning free-hanging art quilts

Art quilts are generally not designed to be washed and yet, like anything, they can become soiled over time.

To prevent unnecessary soiling, don't allow people to touch your quilt! For many, this can be a temptation too strong to resist as other quilters (and non-quilters) will be fascinated to examine the stitching and the back of the quilt.

Sadly, some people don't stop to think of the consequences this may have.

So how should you clean an art quilt?

What type of materials are used in the quilt?

First take a look at its construction:
- What fabrics are used? These could range from quilting cottons to wool, linen, nylon, polyester, paper, plastic, metal—anything goes!
- Does it have beads or other 'found' items attached to the surface?
- Does it have hand-painted details?
- Does it have loose items or thread? Fringes or tassels?

Cleaning

The materials, and construction techniques of an art quilt largely determines how it should be cleaned.

An art quilt that has acquired a soil spot or small stain *may* be able to be sponged with a clean sponge moistened with cold water. However, you should first determine if this is going to damage the quilt in any way.

The best way to clean an art quilt is to **vacuum** it. Lie the quilt down on a flat, clean surface and, using the upholstery or brush attachment on your vacuum cleaner, and the lowest power setting, gently move across the quilt to vacuum up dust and other particles.

If you don't have an upholstery attachment for your machine, place a piece of sheer polyester fabric or nylon stocking over the vacuum nozzle to prevent the nozzle sucking up the fabric or embellishments.

Take care to avoid rubbing or dislodging any surface embellishment such as threads, beading, buttons or loose stitching.

If your art quilt has become very soiled and requires wet cleaning, take it to a professional textile conservator.

Cleaning framed art quilts

Quilts framed under glass—especially UV glass—require little care that you would not afford a valuable painting hanging on your walls.

If the framed work is not protected with glass or Perspex, assess the surface as before, and gently vacuum the quilt face.

6.4 HANGING YOUR QUILT

Hanging a quilt on the wall not only beautifies your home. It also allows people to see your skills first hand! Art quilts should be hung as you would a painting or other work of art.

Most art quilts come with a hanging sleeve attached to the back, into which can be inserted a flat wooden batten, a dowel rod, decorative quilt hanger, or other professional fixture. This then allows the quilt to be hung on the wall using standard picture hooks.

Framed quilts, either behind glass, or uncovered are hung as pictures, using standard picture hooks.

Some people consider that framing a quilt behind glass detracts from the tactile nature of the piece, but it does preserve the quilt well and makes for easy care and hanging. UV glass also protects the quilt from deterioration due to light.

If you are having your quilt professionally framed, try to find a framer who is accustomed to handling fabrics, embroideries, tapestries or quilts, and uses archival framing materials.

Lastly, to prevent fading, avoid hanging your quilt in strong, direct sunlight.

6.5 STORING YOUR QUILTS

Quilts – general

Small quilts are best stored flat, preferably in an acid-free or archival box or drawer.

Protect the quilt with acid-free tissue paper or clean, white, cotton sheeting to shield it from dust and light.

Large quilts:
- Cover the quilt with acid-free tissue or clean, white cotton sheeting.
- Flat storage—place on a clean shelf, drawer, or in a large box, line with acid-free paper.
- Rolled storage—roll loosely with the image side **out**, and place in a cylinder. Keeping the quilt in a cylinder will prevent creases and subsequent fabric stress which can permanently damage the fibers.
- Never fold an art quilt!

The storage area should be dry, dark and have good air circulation.

Avoid high humidity and extremes of temperature.

Antique and Heirloom Quilts

If your quilt is extremely old or valuable, seek professional advice from a qualified textile conservator — ask your local gallery or museum for advice if you're not sure where to start looking for an expert.

Archival storage materials include:
- Acid-free textile boxes.
- Acid-free rolling tubes.
- Polypropylene, lidded boxes.
- Acid-free tissue paper:
    - Buffered Acid-free Tissue for paper, cotton and linen.
    - Unbuffered Acid-free Tissue for wool and silk. Use unbuffered if you are unsure about the materials in your quilt.
- Tyvek—protects against dust, moisture and light.

Conclusion

Taking the time to properly handle, clean, hang and store your precious art quilts will reward you, and generations to come, with beautifully preserved fine art. Think of your children and grandchildren, and how they will cherish the love and detail that has gone into making your quilt, regardless of whether it is an art quilt hung on the wall, a utilitarian quilt in everyday use, or an heirloom quilt that will endure for generations.

Caring for any textile piece requires just a little time and consideration about storage and cleaning.

Just as importantly, the effort and care you have put into creating this artwork is worthy of you showing it the same care once complete.
Your art is worth the effort!

ABOUT THE AUTHOR

Australian textile and digital artist, **Deborah Wirsu,** shares and teaches how to make wonderful thread sketched or thread painted textile art, and art quilts, offering creative ideas, easy-to-follow advice, along with informative tips, tutorials and online classes.

She is the owner and developer of the popular website *Thread Sketching in Action.*

Early forays into a range of sewing and textile arts and crafts led, over time, to a fascination with 'painting' with thread and fabric, creating visually appealing works of art using surprisingly easy-to-master techniques.

As long as you can use a sewing machine, you can learn to draw and paint with thread and fabric.

Her work has been exhibited and sold worldwide, and her passion for teaching online has allowed her to reach out to thousands of students around the globe.

Other business and recreational pursuits involve Classical Music, and Writing, Proofreading and Editing, and living a healthy lifestyle.

Find out more at: www.ThreadSketchingInAction.com

Register today for her FREE Newsletter full of tips, techniques and tutorials.

OTHER BOOKS BY DEBORAH WIRSU

Creative Thread Sketching: A beginner's guide
Available as Print book or Kindle eBook

Printed in Dunstable, United Kingdom